THIS JOURNAL BELONGS TO:

CHECK OUT ALL OF OUR WATERCOLOR DOG JOURNALS SERIES

COLLEGE-RULED LINED JOURNALS
amazon.com/gp/product/B094NQWSPR

DOT GRID JOURNAL NOTEBOOKS
amazon.com/gp/product/B094NTJ2BS

amazon.com/gp/product/B08S2NFGZQ

LOVE IT?

Buy it again or get one for yourself!

Hello and thank you for purchasing this book. We hope you have enjoyed using it as much as we enjoyed designing it. We are a small husband and wife business. Words cannot express how much we appreciate that you bought our book.

It would help us a lot if you could take a moment and leave a review about this book on Amazon.

Pet Lovers Universe

Made in the USA
Middletown, DE
27 February 2023

25824849R00071